THE WINDOWS OF GRACELAND NEW AND SELECTED POEMS

Martina Evans grew up in County Cork, Ireland and has lived in London since 1988. The author of ten books of prose and poetry, Evans's awards include the 2011 Premio Ciampi International Prize for Poetry. *Burnfort, Las Vegas* (Anvil, 2014) was shortlisted for the Irish Times Poetry Now Award 2015, and *Mountainy Men*, a narrative poem, was the recipient of a Grants for the Arts Award in 2015. She is currently Associate Lecturer in Creative Writing at Birkbeck University, London and a Lector for the Royal Literary Fund Reading Round 2014–2016.

D1276783

Martina Evans

THE WINDOWS OF GRACELAND NEW AND SELECTED POEMS

CARCANET

First published in Great Britain in 2016 by Carcanet Press Limited
Alliance House, 30 Cross Street, Manchester, M2 7AQ

www.carcanet.co.uk | info@carcanet.co.uk

All collections represented here were first published by Anvil Press.
These versions of the poems incorporate some revisions by the author and
may be considered authoritative.

A CIP catalogue record for this book is available from the British Library.
ISBN 9781784102760

The publisher acknowledges financial assistance from Arts Council England.

CONTENTS

New Poems

from All Alcoholics Are Charmers

from Can Dentists Be Trusted?

NEW POEMS

FINE GAEL FORM A COALITION GOVERNMENT WITH LABOUR, MARCH 1973

They never seemed close – the old whiskey
Master and the young pastel-lipped teacher.
They shared the same roof over our two-roomed
school, that was all – the dividing door a thick
fifties coral gloss with its six panes of glass,
where their faces would appear if they needed
to summon one another. It wasn't often.
And she must have winced at the howls
that came from his side.
But when they met over his coffee flask
the day after the election, somehow
they couldn't separate. Fine Gael were *in!*
The party of professionals and well-heeled
farmers. Daddy's smile drew a line back to the
twenties, to the Civil War, a victory for *The Big Fella*,
whose eight-by-four photo stood on the mantelpiece
in Daddy's bedroom, Daddy's IRA
medal draped on one corner. I accepted it
then that such good news would drive people
to forget themselves but now I can't
believe the way they forgot us too –
what could the Master have been saying to her
that took so long, was he planning the budget
or choosing the cabinet of the twentieth Dáil?
We weren't called in after the eleven o'clock break
we ran wild for miles, for hours, for weeks,
deep scratches along my thighs, Betty's old sixties
minidress with the pink and orange circles
no protection against the waist-deep briars
in the woods behind the church where everyone
who had them was smoking Carrolls No. 1.
We ransacked rubbish for makeshift hurleys –
anything would do, the boys said but

they banned my old frying pan when they saw
I could run forever with the ball.
I was wearing that light dress so it must
have been summer before it stopped.
All the beatings, the cruelty behind those walls
continued undisturbed but someone
had to put a stop to us roaming like tinkers
when boys were seen riding the roof
of Paddy the Priest's cottage like
it was a horse. And when Mick Looney
passed the graveyard, the crane shot
from his combine harvester showed him
a child sitting on every stone.

WATCH

The night before my wedding
I put my wristwatch through the machine cycle.
It was not in a jeans pocket or tied to a belt,
not wrapped in a T-shirt
nor balled up in a pair of tights.
No. I put it in the empty machine,
shut the door and turned
the wheel of the switch revving the Bosch
to life. Standing nonplussed on the concrete floor
of the bottle shed, it dripped in my hand
after the forty-minute cycle.
I'd been wondering what
was inside and then I remembered
like I was watching someone else
bending to place the watch inside the drum
carefully, like a bundle of delicates
turning the dial like a sleep-walker.
I could hear the clink of glasses
and murmur from the bar as
I went out into the dark and stars
of the backyard to take
the futile action of hanging
the glittering face by its worn strap
from the clothesline
up to my ankles
in wet grass.

MY PERSEPHONE

Was it the small red crab apples crushed flat
making the Holloway pavements flush
with their trees' harvest, the brown leaves

on the ground, the bombed conkers,
the fact I was ten days late
that made me think she was Persephone?

I already knew her sex, despite my best intentions,
the temptation of working in X-ray – I'd spread the gel,
scanned the shadowy form, turning prettily.

Now it was 3 p.m. on the day. I'd been in labour since 2 a.m.
but he'd wanted to have lunch with his cousin (and drinks).
Go, I said. Who wants a man who wants to be elsewhere?

I made a Mr Guinness cake which wouldn't bake
in the centre, hopping around the yellow kitchen
with the skewer, as the cramps tested me.

I packed a suitcase full of books and pens and papers
I rang my sister about the vomiting.
Could it be a stomach bug? She wondered.

I rang the Whittington, they weren't taking us
serious either. You've plenty time, Sister Murphy said an hour
before she said I was too dilated, too late for the epidural

I'd been persuaded was a must for a nervous person
like myself who was writing a poem about Persephone
during the second stages of labour and Pluto was –

where else? – down below in the pub.

EVERYTHING INCLUDING THIS ROOM IS A FUTURE RUIN

And when the wind is finished
with us, the rain starts.
I think it will never

stop – worried
by cracks in the wall and
the lump of dislodged lead

that is directing
the rain down into the brick
so that a tobacco-coloured

liquid drips down
the inside of the window
and some strange yellow

cauliflowers are growing
inside the kitchen walls.
In 1999 I slept high

in the bird's nest
Marcel and Alice were
kittens and the night after

I took up the fragmenting
1970s carpets, their paws
thundered on the floorboards

frightening me. Now
2014, I've gone to ground
like a badger in the basement

to be close to the garden,
and the sounds
have changed as the cats jump

from table to floor over
my head and pass in and
out the flap a dozen times.

I hold my heart again.
Donny growls low
in his ginger belly and I see

the fox so close,
his brown-fawn face
like a friend's and it is hard

to see him run from us,
his bare rump –
something's made his fur fall

out and he runs up the spiral
staircase and I run to the backdoor.
I want to welcome him

but he is on the fence and
then Martin's galvanised roof
and gone.

OYSTERS

It feels good everyone says so,
warm and small like a doll's
house and because it never housed
anyone with the money to exercise change
all the fireplaces intact
and the eight-paned internal window
of the basement bedroom
looking into the low hallway,
(although the concrete floor must
have been mud before) and
the garden earth full of artefacts –
pram wheels, green glass, china, milk
bottle tops, monstrously thick
broken crockery
and seam after seam of oyster shells
because that's what they ate,
washed down with stout
the pastrycook assistants,
butcher boys and nursemaids who
lived in these poor rooms
with their grand pretensions
all decked out in miniature,
the *piano nobile* windows
on the first floor, the laughable
appropriate architraving
for servants and their betters
and yet at night when
I hear certain noises and the cats stare
when the picture of Our Lady
of Guadalupe is transported
by the optical illusion of the Camden Passage
lamp and the eight panes of glass
to hover over the narrow basement stairs
despite all my childhood fantasises
of time travel and poking Henry the Eighth

in his fat sectarian brocade
with my future finger,
I am afraid
I'll see them:
so small and sickly pre-
penicillin pus-filled
not clean and the smell.
I imagine them like the Irish fairies
low-sized, half-human, queer-looking.
I've never liked oysters
on the table either
rough and slithery
dirty-looking
and capable of killing you
like some awful nineteenth-century disease
like general paralysis of the insane,
like syphilis.

THE IRISH AIRMAN PARACHUTES TO EARTH

'For wisdom is the property of the dead,
A something incompatible with life; and power,
Like everything that has the stain of blood,
A property of the living...'

W. B. Yeats, 'Blood and the Moon'

I know that I shall meet my fate
somewhere near the ground.
Perhaps the basement where
I sleep now. I can't see
the moon there except in June
when it rides so low I put
my two rough gardening hands
on the window frame, peering
out to the left where it appears
between two buildings and I can't
decide if it's flashing a signal
or trying to hide.
The cats circle me, in courtly fashion
leaping in and out through
the green curtains onto the sill,
specially softened for them
with pink and grey Mexican blankets.
Their pupils fill with black to allow
more light while the roses glow white
over the crepuscular giant shadows
of the castor oil plant.
I don't think the cats look at the moon.
I think they just happen to glance
in that general direction.
All they want is to be told –
like my father told his cats
with his rough hand,
the light touch of his crooked fingers on their fur –
that they are not alone,

that they are important,
as for being wise,
it's hard to be sure.
Even cats are surprised into falling,
fooled by shadows,
blindsided.

UNICORNS

for Liane Strauss

'But this animal does not figure among the barnyard animals, it is not always easy to come across, it does not lend itself to zoological classification. Nor is it like the horse or bull, the wolf or deer. In such circumstances we may be face to face with a unicorn and not know for sure that we are. We know that a certain animal with a mane is a horse and that a certain animal with horns is a bull. We do not know what the unicorn looks like.'

Jorge Luis Borges

It's a great comfort to know that we can't
know them and so the two I have outside
in the garden can rest assured I won't tell
anyone although I'm telling you now and
they have many disguises, bleached white
in a hot May, coy behind the bluebells
they are pretending to be white horses with one spike each
where the plaster fell off their left ears – how did
that happen? The exact same thing to each one?
That's no coincidence. In the rain
their peeled patches darken and they're like Tinker
Piebalds or Indian Palaminos. Broken and thrown
out of a grand house in Hampstead
to lie in the salvage yard next to Mr Allsorts'
shop and we'd just come to a turn
after a stack of Butler sinks and an old toilet
painted with lotuses when Liadain cried out and
I was sure that she was right – Look, two unicorns.
I didn't have the price of a bus fare that day
but I asked the man to put them away for us.

WUTHERING HEIGHTS

for Kraige Trueman

It's never far away from me despite
being no longer young or romantic
and when Dora runs free across the pergola
she reminds me more of Kate Bush
than a Norwegian Forest Cat.
It was the darkness
that captured me years ago:
Lockwood in his oaken Georgian bed
the sliding panels like a coffin
Cathy calling outside
the cruelty of her arm sawn across the glass.
Even in my dreams last night when Liadain
came down to the basement
frantic to tell me that someone was
calling and knocking in the back garden
outside my casement window
and even in my stark terror when I lifted
my head from under the covers
in the lightening room –
which I could see was empty now
except for Dora's shaggy silhouette –
I couldn't help asking the dream-Liadain
even though I knew the real Liadain
was still asleep in her own room.
Was it like Wuthering Heights?

SHAKESPEARE KNEW CATS

'What, drawn, and talk of peace! I hate the word
as I hate hell, all Montagues, and thee'

He is not complimentary, no doting
Facebook snapper, a man of his time when
it comes to the feline, one weird sister has
Greymalkin and Bendedick says, *Hang me
in a bottle like a cat and shoot me* while Tybalt
is the Prince of Cats. If we hadn't named
the usurping Burmese from De Beauvoir Road,
The Viper, because of his threatening neck
moves, he would be Tybalt. *Do you bite your
thumb at me sir? no, I do not bite my thumb
at you, sir but I bite my thumb, sir.* Off it kicks
as Donny-Romeo leaps in defence – *You lie!*
I run below the high fence imploring like Benvolio,
*part fools, put up your swords you know not what
you do!* to all I can see of Donny-Romeo
his tail bloated with rage, deaf to me, roaring,
*it fits when such a villain is a guest.
I'll not endure him.* The ladies on the balcony,
Dora and Alice rise on their hind legs to watch
the show, the gold and green of their eyes
vanishing into dark pupils *burning like coals*
as the toms crash along the honeysuckled pergola,
giant eyes fixed on one another. *This stupidity
will come back to bite you*, Donny-Romeo. Fang
to fang is no *holy palmer's kiss* – it is life and death
when teeth carry poison that but one month ago
made your ginger cheek round as an orange.
AIDS and feline flu' are passed freely over
these garden walls and Viper-Tybalt
is impervious to the water weapon.
Hose and rattling steel buckets have I used
on him while he stands his dripping ground

like a princox, a saucy boy. Wilful choler makes him
shake and I am helpless as before my own wilful
self. This like everything human will be played
out on the hormones, I won't be given a say
until I'm nursing Donny-Romeo, dealing
with the *bitterest gall*, the veterinary bill,
broken bones.

from

ALL ALCOHOLICS ARE CHARMERS

1998

BACON AND CABBAGE

He said that it was a fact.
The whole field to be turned
into a small village
with our own roads, post office,
sweetshop to include toys.
No adults.
Their head wouldn't get in the doors.
Brothers and sister would live together
and never go off to get married.
The boys would go fishing
and the girls could come too,
if they didn't want to stay behind
baking apple tarts.
There would be no more bacon and cabbage.
No one would stand for it.
Connemara ponies would do all the work
and it would only take an hour a week.
I only had to send in my order
and my bed would be teeming with pups.
When I asked was it really really a fact,
he shouted, had I not heard the priest
announce it off the altar on Sunday?
I hadn't because I never listened anyway.
But I couldn't believe
that Father O'Shea would make such final remarks
about bacon and cabbage.

THE MOBILE LIBRARY

It came once a fortnight
and I went under the bed
scrabbling for overdue books,
balls of fluff and mice skating
across the linoleum.

It parked at the cross
for I don't know how long
and sometimes if I wasn't ready
with the books, I'd look out
and it would be gone.

Why didn't you tell me sooner?
I'd run out breathing anxious breaths
that tasted like frozen lemonade.

And that was the best thing
when I knew that it was still there,
my feet pressing into the deep steps.

THE BLACK PRIEST

He came
to examine us in religion.
His skin wasn't black,
just the hair on his head,
the back of his neck,
his hands, his wrists.

His shaved chin blue
like a pirate's, he came
from an island
some giant Irish-speaking
race that made him huge
and us helpless.

The sound of his name,
an t-Aithair Ó Súilleabháin
had a ring of wildness
to it, made us sit up.

It was hard to pretend
our normal indifference
with his big legs doubled up
in the nun's chair. Someone
next to me whispered that
his knees were like rockets.

But I didn't answer.
From where I was sitting
I could see Sister Lazarian
an arrangement
of dark folds of cloth
in the corner, quivering
waiting for one of us
to break out.

ONE EVENING IN JULY

From a convent to a boat
and straight down
to Ward's in Piccadilly
with my big sister.

I was sitting on a barrel
when a Glaswegian beckoned
and I leaned forward
while he whispered
in my ear.

Something good
I didn't doubt, weren't
the Scots and the Irish
mad about each other?

I'm looking forward
to the twelfth, he said.
I nodded knowingly.
I'm going over
for the twelfth, he said
again and I tried to
think of something
encouraging.

The weather might hold out,
I said. Listen here, Fenian
bitch, he said and I put
my hand over my mouth.
I'm going over to kill
your brothers and sisters.

But my family don't live
in the North, I said,
whipping him up
when it was the last thing
I wanted to do.

I thought the Fenians were all dead,
I said, nearly put my hand out
to feel that he wasn't a ghost.

Papist was the next queer
word he came out with
and he ran out, looking awful
upset before I had time
to tell him that I'd just recently
become an atheist.

ALL ALCOHOLICS ARE CHARMERS

All alcoholics
are charmers
my mother said
that is if
they are any good.
How else would
they get away
with it?
Your father
for instance.
Don't mention
my father,
I said.
He's had a
terrible sad life.
Listen to that
for twisting,
she said,
I was the one
with the
terrible sad life.
How could he have
the time for it,
when he was on the
road day and night?

All alcoholics
are charmers.
If they're any good.
That's how they get
away with it.
My father wore a soft
grey overcoat
with a soaking smell

of smoke and whiskey.
Made me want
to hang onto it
like a blanket.
When he was dying,
my mother was always
crying and waving
a bottle of Black Bushmills
just out of his reach.

All alcoholics
are charmers.
My father gave up
the drink
every single Lent
no matter how
they coaxed.
You can say
what you like,
you can nail me
to the cross,
he said,
nothing
will persuade me
to take anything
stronger
than a good warm glass
of Sandyman's Port Wine.

COWS

are mostly silent,
sharp-shouldered,
fertile,
moist-eyed,
long-lashed,
cream-coloured,
or black,
or black and white,
or brown,
or brown and white,
or red,
or red and white,
(white with red ears
the ones from the
underworld),
motherly,
slow-walking,
vegetarian,
horny
and gentle,
all women dread
to be called
cows.

CHRISTMAS DAYS

After Mass, he was at the gate.
I don't know who he was.
He might have been one of the brothers dressed up.
1949. We all went down to the gate, right?
I was given a big box. I couldn't believe it.
Inside the box, lovely box.
I opened it, train carriages, you know with the tracks, right?
And we got our presents and we opened it.
And then the brothers said, Now boys, time for your dinner.
Line up, please.
Christmas dinner on the table.
When we came back the presents weren't there.
We never saw them no more.
I only saw it for ten minutes.
I never seen it no more.
The next year.
It was brushes and a bucket.
And all the little colours, yellow, pink, orange.
That was 1950. It was in a set.
Big brushes, that length –
all little bottles, full of colours, red and blue.
That was 1950.
Same thing happened, went to your dinner.
Never saw it again, never seen it no more.
1951, one of the boys said and one of the brothers heard him,
we won't see this no more.
He got a hiding, a good hiding.
He was put to bed wrapped in a mackintosh with no food.
That was what they did to me when I wet my trousers in Benediction.
They put me in bed for a day in a mackintosh.
It was sort of red-looking.
They took the sheets and the blankets off the bed.
That was 1951.
I still remember the carriages I was given.
And the tracks. 1949.

I was trying to use the paints.
We left all our presents on the table.
We never saw them no more.
That's true. Where did they go?
Did they sell them or what?
I'm talking about the forties here.
We seen it, they were new all right.
They were brand new.
But where did they go?
Where did the train set go in 1950?
Paints, the tubes, all the little colours, red and orange and all?
After Mass every Christmas Day, Santa Claus down at the gate.
We all rushing down to the gate. Here's Santie, right?
You go to your Christmas dinner that day.
And where did they go from the table?
Who took them while we were eating our Christmas dinner?

YOUNG MAYO MEN

They're like something
out of *Vogue,* I said
and I was told to put on my glasses.
High noon in Holloway,
they're digging the roads.

Inside, I'm reading
The Soul of Man Under Socialism
by Oscar Wilde.
I've begun to leave the flat
by different routes, I can't bear
the shyness of us all.

How bad would Oscar
have felt, would he
have felt each shovel sound
like a blade in his side?

Oscar would have wanted
to do beautiful things with them.
He would not have wanted
to rush out and say *for god's sake
give me that shovel. Stop shovelling.*

The Mayo accent is being hurled
around under my window, I can't
understand most of it. All I can
make out is the soft-looking one
getting a bit riled
saying over and over
What does it matter?

THE BLACK CAB

From the moment he sat down
she knew he was there,
the yellow death's-head
smiling among the steamy-wet
pile of out-patients.

She prayed she wouldn't get him.

As the afternoon wore through
the shuffling crowd, she feared
that every name she called
would unfold him from his seat.

And she got him in the end,
had to feel the zygomatic arches
under his waxy-skinned cheeks,
stare close into his eyes
as she adjusted his skull.

He never took his smiling eyes
from her face, talking about
the accident,
the drunk and drugged girls,
how she was only seventeen,
the one who came crashing
through his windscreen,
to sit up dead in his lap.

THE TREATMENT FOR CANCER OF THE LIP

It was a radioactive implant,
a big square thing
like a chunk of plug tobacco
sewn into the lower lip.

Old-fashioned smokers
of clay pipes,
now a radioactive source,
had to be kept away
from everyone else,
they fogged X-ray films
and frightened children.

What did they think
these men in flat caps
with their sulky lips,
banished to corners
far away from
Clarke's No. 1 Plug,
Erinmore, Condor
and Cherokee,
to this place
without fire or smoke,
nothing to cut and shape,
or press and hold,
not even a dog for company?

HIS MASTER'S TEETH

The Chinese puppeteer
with the prominent teeth
has the look
of a North Cork bowler.

Country men
had irresistible smiles,
lips that just wouldn't
stay down over their teeth.

Strong arms swinging
round like millwheels,
the mad run down
sighing country roads,
the bawl of spectators,
the whisper of bets.

His delicate yellow-faced
puppet dances with elegantly-
jointed hands and knees,
its old painted face
moving under the twitching
fingers, twitching lips.

Chinese words, Chinese
vowels running alongside
the vowels of men
from Banteer, Kanturk,
Bweeng and Dromahane.

The surge of trees and voices,
Good man, Christy!
The rustle of twenty- and fifty-
pound notes.

GREY MARE

i.m. Thomas Cotter (1900–1979)

After the Truce
his prison letter
was all about
his dream about
her.

Coming first
in the mare and brood class
at Newcastle,
his bursting pride
leading her into the ring
with colours up.

Afterwards,
awake in the cell,
his fear for her leg
was stronger
than his hope
for 'a grand and glorious peace'.

She was the first person he called on
the night of his escape.

In the seventies
he was an old fighter,
the same age as the century
hook nose, burnt brown eyes,
whiskey head, tobacco fingers.

Yellow riding boots
with elasticated sides,
morning or evening,
wedding or funeral
always on his feet.

He was ready for her
the day she'd come again
drumming her hooves.

from

CAN DENTISTS BE TRUSTED?

2004

GAS

Little did I think, nailed by pain
and wandering, squeezing hands
in my first dentist's chair
that I would be running down the road
to my second sea-side dentist
who had great gas in a cylinder.
The third in Munster to have *Relative*
Analgesia, Mr Shinkwin, Clonakilty
didn't believe in suffering.
Cold thin air breathed through a mask
changed everything. He played the drill
like Hendrix – *Johnny Be Good* –
his eyes over his mask,
blazing blue as the Atlantic Ocean
that belted against the side
of this small town. My friend, Dolores
rightly worried that it would come
to the nuns' ears
that the hysterical laughter of a boarder
had been heard out on the street.
But by now, I was in Harts,
still laughing, flashing my silver fillings
examining the jewelled jars and glass cases,
buying quarters and quarters
of sweets.

A BEIGE MINI IN THE SIXTIES

The smallness of it, our bare knees poking out
of our corduroy paisley dresses
and the backs of our legs glued to the warm seats.

The bottle of water for topping up the radiator
that always sat in the side pocket with a bottle of holy water
in the shape of a see-through Virgin Mary.

My brother putting the plastic Virgin to his lips
and drinking down great slugs before driving away
to an exam which he failed anyway.

The crash at the junction of Pine Street and the fuss
that was made of Fifi the dog by the staff in Casualty
at the North Charitable Infirmary.

Waiting outside the Bank of Ireland while she made her lodgement,
dreading the moment we would have to walk up to strangers, 'Excuse me,
my mother's just learned to drive, could you turn our car and face it
for home please?'

Shopping by the sea in Clonakilty,
navy 'wet look' patent shoes for my mother,
red shoes with buckles for me.

Fifi hanging her hairy head out the window,
me hanging my boy's haircut out of the window,
the sweet taste of the gulps of flying air.

My mother driving to Limerick
and getting up on the wrong part of the new road,
workmen running after us, shaking their fists.

My father's face
when my mother put her foot on the accelerator
and told him he was at her mercy.

The cloud of gravel
when she drove out of the yard
and the gasps from the men looking out the window.

I can't remember how the Mini died
only our disgust when she replaced it
with a black Morris Minor for fifty pounds.

She laughed at us and said she didn't care,
she wasn't ashamed of it, she would collect us
from the convent in it, visit us more often in fact.

But in the end the Morris Minor refused to budge, mocked her view
from the kitchen window, stuck to the stones of the rough ground
where the salesman had parked it.

ON LIVING IN AN AREA OF MANIFEST GREYNESS AND MISERY

'London is a vast ocean in which survival is not certain.'

'Essex Road and the unluckily named Balls Pond Road
are areas of manifest greyness and misery.'

Peter Ackroyd, *London: The Biography*

I sleep high on the bird's nest.
Trucks and lorries shake the house
and make the bricks tremble,
roaring tidal waves rock the bed
and put me to sleep.
There are odd wrecked Georgian houses
beached between tyre shops and takeaways.
Sometimes people are murdered.
Police sirens shriek up and down all day
like seagulls chasing sandwiches.
On the second floor,
we can look right into the 38
and see all the people
and we think they can't see us.
And we can jump on the 38 ourselves,
sail on the top deck
down to Bloomsbury and Victoria.
Our walls are stuffed with horsehair,
on stormy nights we hear the horses gallop.
Like us, they don't want to leave.
The ghost of a cat lives next door.
Young black drivers play hip-hop and dance hall,
when they stop it's a five-minute party
and you never know when it might happen.
The pink-haired squatters dance topless
on the concrete roof when it's hot.
John Ball's pond lies under our back gardens,
the shades of his cows low at full moon.

But it's the roll of traffic
that makes it more of an ocean
especially the sound of rushing wheels
when it rains,
and the uniformed Catholic children
slip along the wet pavement
like blue fish
swimming down the Balls Pond Road.

THE DAY MY CAT SPOKE TO ME

for Geraldine More O' Ferrell

I was surprised not so much by the fact
that she spoke
but by the high opinion she had of me.
'I think you're great,' she said
and it was at this point I looked at her
in surprise.
'I mean,' she continued, 'the way
you've managed to write anything at all!
Fourteen court hearings
and that horrible barrister,
the way she looked at you.'
But you weren't there,' I said.
'Oh but I can imagine it,' said Eileen,
her yellow eyes opening wide
before narrowing into benevolent slits.
'I only had to look at you,
gulping down your red lentil soup
when you came home after nearly three
hours in the witness box defending
your right to write.
Did anyone ever hear the like?
I could see it all in every swallow you took,
her butty legs and her manly shoulders
in that black suit, did she have dandruff?
I hope not, because it really shows up on black.
Saying those things to you,
Oh Miss Cotter we would all like the luxury
of sitting at home writing books!
Holding up paper evidence between finger
and thumb *Here is another job*
you failed to get Miss Cotter.

Trying to make you go out to work
with radiation in a hospital
and who would take care of us?
What would the cats of this house
do without the sound of your pen scratching
on paper, the hum of your computer,
your lovely lap and the sound of you
on the telephone?
The big dyed blonde head of her!
And where did she think she was going?
Well, earning a lot of money for her own words
by the looks of things.
And saying them to you!
The best writer that ever heaved a can of Tuna
or opened a pack of Science Plan.
And as Mary Jenkins said about him
who paid for the horrible utterances,
It's just as well that Shakespeare wasn't married to him.
And then when he was in the witness box, he wished
you the best of luck with your writing....'
At this point Eileen paused, closed her eyes
I was waiting for her to say something witty herself.
After all it was a great opportunity for irony
which for some reason I have
always associated with cats.
But when she opened her eyes again
she requested a scoop of softened butter
after which she licked her lips in detail
and hasn't opened her mouth since
if you don't count yawning, lapping,
eating, washing miaowing,
and screeching at intruders.

THE RABACH

It was the father,
the old Rabach
who put him
up to it.

And the Rabach
killed the sailor
who'd come so deep
into the glen,
two hours' walk
from the road.

Under the shadow
of Tooth Mountain,
the sailor came for shelter,
up rocks
as big as carts,
plunging through the bog,
striped slugs and rushes
until the sheer walls
of stone closed him in.

The Rabach hid the body,
under the hearth stone,
leaned out
in the early morning,
to smoke a pipe.

Gatekeepers and painted ladies
skimmed the bog,
grasshoppers gritted
among the purple loosestrife,
spotted orchids
and feverfew.

It was only a scut
of an English deserter
who wouldn't have the gumption
to haunt him.

There could be peace here now
with the pipits and the wagtails,
the sound of that hum
across the bog.

Except why did Mary Sullivan
have to be doing
the good woman
getting up at five
to draw fresh water
for tea?

Tea for her long-nosed
so-and-so of a husband
for his two-day journey,
on a horse too good for him,
to the Butter Exchange in Cork.

The houses were too close
in this stone room of a glen.

She'd seen him
at that hour
through the deep small
square window, blessed
herself and said
nothing.

Until the day
she had a row
with the Rabach
and he pushed her

into the heather
and meadowsweet.

She'd had her warning
that afternoon,
along the side
of the mountain,
stones cast a shadow face
real and hard,
with an overhanging brow.

Yet she couldn't keep it
to herself,
the wet scramble up
from the ground.
His hard blue stare.

I could put you away for good.

He followed her,
choked her with a spancel
and she stared
at the holly tree that grew
out of the cleft
of a rock.

There were no other trees
only rocks and stones.

Upside down in the stream
to make it look like drowning,
she was in no position
to put anyone away for good.

Afterwards he went down
to Glanmore Lake,
rinsed the sweat

off his face and hands.
Smoked another pipe.

The bright, long-bodied
damsel flies were flying
over the rocks,
if he was a scholar
he'd know the word
in Irish to describe
the exact stamp
of that bursting blue.

Damsels were born
as grubs
on the bed
of the lake
had to rise
between the bites
of fishes,
not a whole pile
came through.
There was great heat
there that day,
great comfort in the rays
drying his face.

Some foreign blackguards
had shot the swan's mate,
the Rabach sat on a flat rock
and cried for the one swan
going round and round
the lake,

little knowing
that some big budan
of a copper miner
from Allihies

had been up the hill
and saw him at Mary.

The miner only kept quiet
because he'd been stealing
cows' tails himself,
it was on his death bed
that he started his pillalooing.
Told the priest.

That was when
the Tally Ho started.
A whole year
he was on the run
and it was no joke
up high in a cave,
cold, afraid to light
a fire, sending triple
echoes across the rocks
to scare them off.

Mists came right up
to the mouth
Pluais an Rabach
white veils hanging
like sheets on a line
in front of him.

If he was a couple
of inches taller, he thought,
he'd be able to see right
over the top of them.

The heather changing,
the harebells,
wild bitter apples,
snow, then snowdrops,

bog cotton and the bluebell,
the Virgin Mary's own flower.

Everywhere there were scattered
split and scored rocks and boulders
behind which a hundred men
could hide.

Mary Sullivan's son
was growing up too,
he gave the tip,
knowing the special day
when the Rabach
would be at home
with his wife.

Her labour was hard,
he had to break
a three-legged stool
to keep out the sound
of her pain.

Across the bog,
the soft brown hares
were hopping. They said
that the hares had big giant
cousins in Van Dieman's Land.

You'd see them if you got transported.

Her pain caught him in the throat,
he couldn't even smell the wild flowers
or hide from the blaze of redcoats
that blew up around the house.

He wouldn't look at them
when they tied him.

He kept his two blue eyes fixed
on the holly tree
and on the cracked and scattered
boulders behind which a hundred men
could hide.

They said that he was the last man
to be hanged in Munster,
They said when they opened
him up afterwards,
he had two hearts.

THE ROOM

'When I die I will return to seek
The moments I did not live by the sea'

Sophia de Mello Breyner

It has always been waiting,
long windows down to the dusty floorboards,
golden brown tea as good as I drank
out of pink and white cups
in the Convent of Mercy thirty years ago.
John McCormack on the record player,
hot cross buns and butter,
the ocean below rising in grey sheets
same colour as my coat
which hangs by the door.
In a moment, I put it on,
walk on the sand
with the spray on my face.

BURNING RUBBISH

A peachy sunset
over a line of black fir trees,
fires all over our field.
I am there in shorts and sandals
running with a can of petrol
to revive the drooping flames,
my father's solid body
standing still among the blazes
like a Roman General,
just here, this evening
for once
like a king.

Yes, you have to be very careful what you transfer onto your child.

That's a nervous cough, that is.

It really could be you that is causing that cough, you know.

The child is a barometer of the mother.

Well, when she comes round here, she eats everything on her plate.

Yes, I just visualise his first wife and I find the peace.

Ever since I became a Christian.

I know, yes, really, apparently she was being horrible to Constance.

Have you done the homework?

You absolutely can't be serious! Those potatoes, we never touch them in Brazil, English potatoes we call them. No, she needs sweet potato.

Well, the thing with children is that if they know they have no choice you'd be surprised what they eat.

She is just attention seeking, you have to be careful, she is taking control.

Yes, there is a really interesting book on that. Remind me to lend it to you.

It is very wrong to make her do the violin. These things can't be forced.

No. You have to take control, cover the lit tray, then Eileen will have to go in the garden. So what if she doesn't like muddy paws! Show her who's boss.

I just visualise him in pink and then everything is all right.

You have to rise above it.

Mmmm, I can't believe your bad luck, you must have very bad karma.

Yes, if you look in the Old Testament you will see there is an absolute certainty about Vegans.

If you know your blood group then you can figure out from what phase of evolution you are. For instance, group O, hunter-gatherer, you need to keep away from grains.

Well, if you really like bread, that is actually a sign that you shouldn't be eating it.

Visualise yourself in a long blue cloak with red lining... you are approaching a stream, you've got your bundle of worries. Place it carefully beyond the curtain of water.

I sodding well visualised his ex wife and now her photographs are all over the kitchen table.

Well they are at fault. This school and the people at this school give me the pip.

They are a total bunch of loopy hippies. So flaky.

Well, it is true I couldn't get her in anywhere else.

No, I just pray for peace, I pass the problem onto God.

Oh, I've changed since I have been a Christian.

Mmm, yes, yes, yes. It's all about letting go.

But I have a right to my feelings.

The hell I will forgive. That horrible woman, who does she think she is? I'm going to have a word with her tonight. I am.

What's wrong? Yes, well, did you not know?

The moon is in Scorpio.

Well, it's the best education there is, it's the discipline.

If I had a million pounds I wouldn't pick any other school.

Well, maybe if I had the money, maybe that school in Hampstead.

Oh Father, when we sang Be Thou My Vision!

Don't let her think there's a choice about it. Jesus, if you start off with her thinking that she can get away with not going to Mass, God alone knows where she'll end up!

I just get Jack into that pew, come hell or high water. I give him a big tube of Pringles, it keeps him quiet and by the time he's worked his way down through them, Mass is nearly over.

You see, you have peace of mind, you know they're getting the best education.

Well as Eamon said to me the other night, no one talks about the good Christian Brothers.

Of course there is, there's nothing like seeing your daughter coming down the aisle in her First Holy Communion dress, isn't that right, Father?

Father Flynn with his fecking sandwiches, they think we've nothing else to do. Just because we want to get into the school.

Margaret is down in the Centre every Sunday, roasting chickens for winos, just because she wants to get your man in before he gets stabbed at the Comprehensive. And they're determined to make an accountant of him anyway and why wouldn't they?

So, well, we were determined to find out if she was bringing her to Mass in London and when we brought her up to the cloakroom, Bernie asked and the child didn't know what Mass was.

If she was bringing the child to Mass, they wouldn't have half the problems they have.

So they are driving round in their Volvos with boots full of drink that was bought by the funds, drinking the funds. In their big Volvos!

It would make you mad.

And it's their children who get to be serving on the altar.

It's no trouble, Father, so like ten rounds of ham and ten rounds of egg, will that be enough?

Well, Maureen is a teacher, she knows what is suitable for a child and it's not all this spoiling. She told me herself what she would do.

Isn't it desperate? As if it was bad enough with the pair of them split up, but those grandparents will never see her coming down the aisle in a white communion dress.

In any kind of white dress, probably. And never see an altar again, either.

It's the grandparents who suffer the most and I'd know being a grandmother.

Ah, it's very sad, but as I said, if there's alcohol involved. There isn't a chance. Pity, she waited until she was nearly forty.

So they stole the funds and now Father Tom is all over the tabloids and to think I was down there clearing his garden for him, yes Father and No Father and himself and the secretary at it the whole time.

I nearly had a hernia getting into that school.

What's she going to do now she's taken the child out?

But it's a shame, it's a shame, half of it isn't they can't be bothered to put themselves out. Too lazy to go to Mass.

I had to pay Aisling two pounds a week to get her to go to the Communion classes and I couldn't even tell you how much the dress cost.

But now we have the video and no one can take that away from us.

I burst into tears when I heard the organ starting up Be Thou My Vision and didn't I start off again at the reception? I couldn't help it when Father Flynn thanked me again for the sandwiches in front of everybody.

FORTY-FIVE

My head eventually grew
over the top
of the biscuit and white
formica table in the bar
and I could see them there
playing forty-five.

Big red hands with cuts
and grazes and crumpled
fingers, clutching cards
that had to be slammed
to the table with thumps
and cracks of bone
and *hah*s of triumph.

I, too,
wanted to have a blazing face
when I threw down the
gauntlet of a Joker or a five,
and in the winter dark evenings
Tom Twomey, Bill Drummy
and Paddy the Priest played
Beggar my Neighbour, Old Maid
and even forty-five with me.

I was ignorant
of the crucial fact
that gabbing
was worse than reneging,
but they listened, even laughed
and played politely,
keeping their energies
for the evening feast.

Then I hid out
on the windowsill
wrapping
the red velvet curtains
round me
like an Angel
that would appear
in a biblical land,
peering out at a world
of passion and precision
I could not understand.

Set jaws, spellbound fists,
gleeful flings,
blue eye after blue eye
after brown eye,
all holding their whist.
Angel Gabriel could have come
and blown his trumpet off,
the Second Coming
could have come and gone,
they wouldn't have heard a thing.

CAN DENTISTS BE TRUSTED?

There are the ones
you only visit once,
like the fellow
in Phibsboro, Dublin
who roared *Jesus Fucking Christ*
his leg up on the dentist's chair
as he pulled out
my embarrassed tooth.

Or the one who told me to lie
about being pregnant
so I could have crowns
that I never said
I wanted
free on the NHS.

The man in Kensington
who told me he loved
the Irish, really
then died five years later
leaving me the legacy
of a HIV test.

Others, you have to stay with.
But if they are private
they may want all your teeth
in the end
you could find yourself
opening wide
while laid out on the chair
like a corpse
with a gold coin
in its mouth
travelling towards the
underworld.

from

FACING THE PUBLIC

2009

TWO HOSTAGES

In the photo
six bouncing babies, bonneted, sitting
in a pram outside Hackney Workhouse: 1902.
This was the year my father was born.
I have held his powder-blue
vaccination certificate issued
in that year by what was later
considered an alien government.
Could any of these babies come out of Hackney
to put on the Black and Tan uniform?
Bomb us now was the sign on the Crossley Tender,
their bayonets pointed at my father
his hands tied over his head
his thin eighteen-year-old body swaying
against the wire netting of the truck
as it drove past my grandmother
who must have remembered,
as she looked up startled,
all those days she carried him
bonneted, protected in her arms.

In 1921 my two-year-old mother
toddling outside my other grandmother's shop
was picked up by another Crossley Tender.
And this grandmother pursuing the truck
down the long village street
knew that these hated men from the trenches
had shot children
and old men working in the fields
dragged a priest by a rope for sixty miles
wrecked homes never once forgetting
to crush the pictures of the Virgin
and the Sacred Heart under their heel.
They came like pirates with patches over their eyes

hooks instead of hands, tormented minds
tormenting the people they hunted like game
as they drank, swore, swaggered, cocked their pistols
and made the people kneel to sing
God Save the King.
How could she even breathe now as she stopped
outside Sheehy's pub, going inside
to discover my mother sitting on the counter
like a queen, drinking red lemonade
surrounded by those same dark faces
queuing up like suitors,
one of them claiming that he couldn't *get over*
the brown eyes of the Irish
and as my grandmother reported afterwards,
every single word out of his mouth
spoken in the language of Cockney.

THE BOY FROM DURRAS

Yes, that's right, the Tans picked up children
and you know why of course, don't you?
They were looking for information.
I'll tell you something now on the quiet
and you'll get no one round here
to talk about it. No, they wouldn't open their mouths.
There was a young fellow picked up outside Durras.
He was sent down from the house. I'd say only about twelve or thirteen,
not much more, sent down to the shop to get the messages.
And the Tans picked him up, gave him a lift to the shop.
Whether he said something or not was never known.
There's no point in asking me
and you won't get anyone round here to talk about it.
There was an IRA safe house raided that night, anyway
a truck load of the Boys taken to Bandon Barracks.
Well, you wouldn't want to be arrested by the Essex Regiment no sir,
fingernails pulled off and a slow death by the barracks fire –
they were very fond of the red hot poker, the Essex were.
Did the boy give them a tip-off? No one knows.
You'll get no one round here to talk about it today.
And it's seventy years on.
No, a crowd from the village came for the boy.
The parents couldn't save him, he was tied to a horse
and cart and dragged, yes the very same that the Tans
done to that priest outside Dunmanway, he was dragged
as far as Dromore before they stopped.
I'd say that's a distance of about forty mile.
And don't forget that you never heard this from me.

Never trust a Palatine or a Bastard –
and Ould Fritz was both.
When 'the Boys' went to Ould Fritz
demanding their guns in the name of the Irish Republic –
I'll give you ammunition says Ould Fritz,
sticking his gun out of the window.
He shot Joe Bennett stone dead.
Bang. No more than he was a dog.
They wrapped his body in a sheet
put it in a ditch two miles from his home place
because the Tans were down to the house straight.
The Bennetts killed a pig, letting on nothing –
if the Tans found a corpse
they'd be burnt to the ground.
Mrs Bennett, standing there, stuffing sausages
her seventeen-year-old son's body lying in a ditch.
No more than he was a dog.
Those fellas going round the house
sticking their bayonets into everything.
Ould Fritz? Well he didn't leave his house
for fear of the Boys, two whole years getting
everything delivered and everyone laughing
at the big head of him inside the windows.
Of course they got him,
didn't he have to leave the house for his sister's funeral?
All the gentry assembled below in Askeaton Graveyard.
Bang. No more than he was a dog.
Four black horses with feathers going one way
and the hearse going the other.

OMAR KHADR

There is video evidence of Omar at twelve,
wiring explosives laid out like cakes on a tablecloth,
his brown face young under his white kufi,
little boy fingers winding the wire,
white teeth biting the thread
before he was captured
at fifteen, in the broken-biscuit dust
of a blasted Afghan compound
exit wounds on his chest spreading
and red as blooming poppies.
They won't treat his wounds
until he talks, someone has to sing
for the twin towers and Canada won't
extradite him, his family a national
embarrassment, Jihadic mother and
sister speaking out of raven black cloth,
ticking off what every boy should learn –
swimming, sniping, and horseback riding.
In Guantánamo, it's stress positions, orange jump
suits, interrogators calmly recording him
crying out for his mother.
When he's finally asked what he wants
he says car magazines, colouring books
and pencils, any kind of juice
as long as it is really weird.

COURT WELFARE OFFICER

Your teacher said we could talk in the café,
it is a marvellous building isn't it?
Aren't you lucky to be going to a school like this?
Purdy's for you and a tea for me.
You like Purdy's, do you?
Isn't that ceiling marvellous?
You know the restoration work here is an inspiration.
Mmm. Well!
So why don't you want to see your father?
You just don't want to, is that what you are saying.
Just you don't want to.
Well, you were all talk when I met you at home on Tuesday.
How come you can't say anything now?
You are afraid of him?
You'll have to tell me more than that.
I have to tell the judge more than that, you know.
I can't understand why you've gone so quiet.
You were all talk yesterday about your drama class.
The judge will bend over backwards to get you to see him.
You know that, don't you?
You will have to go into a room with him.
What's not safe about it?
It's nothing to worry about, I'll be there too.
You have got to say more than you are saying if you want me
to take you seriously.
Do you know it is your dad who pays the school fees?
He told me himself, yesterday.
He is very sad and I feel very sorry for him.
Yes, I think it's very sad that you won't see him when he is paying the fees.
Look at that beautiful ceiling and the stained glass windows.
Drink up, now. I have to go soon.
I can't go back to the judge and tell him nothing, you know.
It's not fair, the judge will say I am not doing my job properly.
You need to finish up that drink.
You must have something more to say.
I will be told that I am not doing my job properly.
And you will have to leave your drink behind you.

A MAN'S WORLD

He could not bear it – a convent funeral,
his female relatives had to chivvy him along.
His cousin Sister Lazarian laid out
in a sky-blue Child of Mary cloak
with a face like a hawk sticking out
of the coffin. The slippery polished floors,
the green crochet-covered bell rope
hanging like a rebuke in the gloom.
He did not go to Mass.
The tapestries, embroidered swans on cushions
pictures of bishops and saints, tea and sandwiches.
There would be *No smoking*.
And yet, the pale eager faces of the nuns –
down the clean corridors the black habits swirled
and skirled. He knew it was a party
when the fine white fingers poured Scotch
into a heavy glass right up to the top.
Asking questions about the races,
Tipperary's chances in the All Ireland.
In this purified atmosphere
he was an interesting man
with an interesting smell.
He lit a Sweet Afton and flicked ash
into the hand-held ashtray beside him,
sat back as the coiffed and veiled women
arranged themselves around the room
preparing to be mesmerised.

ROYALTY

'It was Jim McMahon who first pointed out
that you never come across a bald tinker,
nor do you ever see one in old age.'

Bernard O'Donoghue

For pure glamour, in my mind
no one could or will
beat the tinkers.
They were outsiders for a start,
sartorial smart, with an edge,
like the dangerous whiff
of burnt rubber you get at the Bumpers.
The young men, sometimes small,
always slim in leather jackets,
torn denim before it became *de rigueur*,
had unforgettable names
like Elvis O'Donnell
Christy O'Driscoll the Bowler.
Even when I was ten
every one of them called me ma'am.
The older men, Teds or Rockers,
sported the side locks of Victorian cads,
with rubbery Native American skin
hair dyed blonde, they drove low
windowless vans and knew everything
about antiques and horses.
They were champion bowlers,
they spoke their own ancient language.
Even the people who abhorred them,
barred them from pubs and shops,
would stop sometimes to whisper
in tones of mystified respect:

See that fellow over there
with the big head of white hair
he's the King of the Tinkers.

COWBOYS

They came with a horse box
a present for Daddy they said,
as he followed them into the bar.
Captain Lyley's face plummy with drink,
Uncle Tommy in shades of brown
and beige, his nicotine fingers, tan ankle boots,
Fry's Chocolate Cream tie.
I circled the yard in excitement, would I be throwing
my leg over a horse, soon? Billy the Kid lepping on
after bursting out of Lincoln Jail.
Taut and grave, I was more like Pat Garrett when
I stole near the box in my sandals,
my hat hanging down my back on its string.
Shouldn't a horse whinny or paw the ground with spirit?
Shouldn't I be able to see the points of her ears
as she tossed her head above the opening?
I pressed my own ear against the petrol-smelling wood.
Soft breathing and slight shifting,
maybe she was a Shetland.
Overhead the crows circled like buzzards.
The yard was deserted, it could have been *High Noon*
but it was dark when they finally came out of the bar
and Uncle Tommy fumbled with the bolts.
A little Dexter cow he announced to myself and Daddy.
The small donkey-brown figure stood
timid and still in the dim light of the BP pump.
Off to one side, Captain Lyley had Mammy's hands
in both of his, saying *Mrs Cotter, I am loath to leave you.*
No one noticed Daddy and me. Our murderous looks.

JAUNTY

Light strikes the clock!
I've waited five hours
for you to come
crashing in,
apologising,
kissing my feet,
and jaunty.

Jaunty! I'll give you
jaunty – I've waited
while my mouth dried up –
a wrinkled raisin of fear –

saw the crash
put you in the ambulance
attended the funeral
bawled at the grave
comforted the orphan
collected the insurance –
all these long clock ticking hours
till you came in,
apologising,
kissing my feet,
and jaunty.

DESPERATE MEN

Christmas Day and Good Friday
were the only days that the pub closed.
And yet they came –
trembling strangers, under hats and caps,
lapels turned up against the slanting wind
or hiding a dog collar. They were desperate.
We knew men like them for 363 days of the year
apologetic, obsequious and persistent,
dark ravens
tap tap tapping at our front door.
Isn't it a fright? everyone whispered
over the Brussels sprouts, *the one day in the year.*
Wouldn't you think they would stock up or their wives could...?
I pondered but *sshhh in the name of God*
my mother looked at me as if I was planning my future.
You'll draw them in on top of us.
She passed out slices of turkey on tip-toe
and we avoided the noise of cutlery on china
chewing tensely until we heard the sound
of footsteps on gravel again
the wind-up growl of an old Escort
or Cortina starting up,
driving away.

CONVERT

When Captain Lyley told the Canon
he was thinking of converting
the ecclesiastical carpet was rolled
right out. Talks at the presbytery
over sherry, the horsey priest nodding
away, hardly able to believe his luck,
the captain confessing to a feeling –
something missing in his life –
impressed by the deep faith of his Catholic neighbours –
these neighbours whose heads craned now
to see him at Mass, spreading out his silk handkerchief
before going down on one knee, sniffing incense,
ceremoniously folding ebony rosary beads
back into his empty wallet.
The captain had three horses to sell
and six weeks was just long enough
for the Canon to buy the mare,
arrange a good price for the other two.
Six weeks for the captain to realise that
he didn't have it in him after all – time
for the Canon to find out who'd really
been biting at the end of the line.

FACING THE PUBLIC

My mother never asked like a normal person, it was
I'm asking you for the last time, I'm imploring you
not to go up that road again late for Mass.

She never had slight trouble sleeping, it was
Never, never, never for one moment did I get a wink,
as long as my head lay upon that pillow.

She never grumbled, because *No one likes a grumbler,*
I never grumble but the pain I have in my two knees this night
there isn't a person alive who would stand for it.

She didn't just have an operation; she died in the Mercy Hospital
and came back to life only when Father Twohig beckoned
from the foot of her blood-drenched bed.

She didn't just own a shop and a pub, she told bemused waitresses
that she was *running a business in the country, urgently*
when she insisted that we were served first.

She didn't do the Stations of the Cross
she sorrowed the length and breadth of the church.
And yet, she could chalk up a picture in a handful of words

conjure a person in a mouthful of speech; she took off her customers
to a T, captivating us all in the kitchen,
drawing a bigger audience than she bargained for.

How often we became aware of that silent listener
when he betrayed himself with a creak, a sneeze or a cough.
How long had he been standing, waiting in the shop?

We looked at each other with haunted faces,
and I, being the youngest, got the job of serving him
his jar of Old Time Irish, his quarter pound of ham,

writing his messages into The Book, red-faced and dumb
before his replete and amused look.
Meanwhile, inside, my mother held a tea towel to her brow.

Never, never, never would she be able, as long as she lived,
even if she got Ireland free in the morning,
no, no, no she would never be able to face the public again.

IVY ON THE WALL

Four storeys high, a foot,
even a foot and a half thick
in some places, green, glossy
and when the wind passed through
you could hear the sea. *Listen, listen to it,*
I kept saying. It was at a time when nothing
would grow for me
nothing except that wall of green.
But in the end, it had to go, and the man
I hired to cut the root turned away, cried,
said that he was sick to his stomach.
As if the vet had broken down
in the middle of putting down the cat,
as if I had asked the man to cut the heart
out of Snow White. I helped him carry
the thick trunk, branches like arms and legs
some as thick as thighs, we were murderers.
The leaves are turning brown now, it is dying,
although at night-time they could pass for green.
Last night, I lay on the ground on my back
and the shifted view made it look like a field
or a fairytale steep thicket,
almost a miracle, except for the TV
aerial that forms a steel cross,
a grave marker
at the top.

If I have to cook Christmas dinner again
I will go off my head! But all she did was rattle
cutlery in the background, tell long winding stories.
It was my sisters' and sisters-in-law's woolly backs
that bent over the roast and the potato croquettes.
God, I can't stand Christmas, she said as she
avoided the decorating and even Daddy
ran away when we asked him
to cut down a Christmas tree. He slapped the naked
turkey and laughed when Ber and I said
we couldn't bear the pimpled flesh.
Well, I have to have a lie down anyway. She went
away with a Stations of the Cross face after dinner
leaving us miserable stuffed turkeys
down in the dark and shuttered bar.
I put the ball of my fist in my mouth when Rhett
told Scarlett he frankly didn't give a damn
and the light from the black and white telly
flickered across our faces.
Come on, throw on your things! She'd be standing
there then with no respect for the television,
her tweed coat swinging open and the keys jangling
in her hand. We walked the bare
North Cork roads under skeletal trees,
saw the rowan, the wren and the fox.
Thanks be to God I've put another Christmas dinner
behind me – it's over, it's over at last!
Up the empty Island Road,
past the odd smoking chimney.

THE KING IS DEAD

The deep Radio Luxembourg voice announced it
like it was an ad for a film. And then
it was *Blue Suède Shoes* and *Return to Sender*
 and the voice again, saying it like that
The King is Dead.
I'm in the old dining room, peering down
at the bar where a few voices flow under one loud one.
Do they know? *The King is Dead*.
They don't know. I could be the one
to announce it. I could walk down into the bar now
and say it: *The King is Dead*. But they might say
I am stupid or that I am trying to be smart
which I am, of course.
The first one in Burnfort to break the news –
who do I think I am? *Love Me Tender*.
I touch the worn velvet tablecloth,
the tin cash box, the plastic fruit.
The King is Dead. I start my journey
but stop by the box of penny bars in the shop.
Retreat, unwrapping a raspberry split.
Look at my face in the brown sideboard mirror.
I've been told I'm wrong so often,
I don't believe my ears
peeping through my long hair.
And besides, that voice – *The King is Dead*
the voice of a salesman if ever I heard one.
Thinning voices as the last people drift away
to the noisy hint of washing glasses,
the bolts running home. I mount the stairs
thinking of how I've missed my chance
and wake in the morning
to my mother's announcement
that the whole world is talking about it.

I don't know why, maybe she needed me as a witness but for some reason, Ber brought me downstairs to the bathroom in the early hours. We turned right two thirds of the way down the staircase, passed in front of the long mirror, where the staircase separated, three steps down to stand in our bare feet on the cold moist red tiles in front of the open frosted window. *Here Brownie, Brownie, Brownie, come on Brownie, Brownie Brownie.* I shivered in my yellow bri-nylon night-dress as he half-ambled, half-wriggled his way up to the window where it opened onto the yard; his belly close to the ground and his head even lower, the shamed look he had when his brown eyes met her brown eyes. She beat him then and there and her hand must have been burning and it seems to me her tears were burning, too, but I couldn't have known that for surely it wasn't I that was crying? And surely, I was thinking, as she must have been thinking, that he would learn his lesson now: *Keep away from those other dogs.* They were the *wrong crowd, a bad influence.* Sooner or later he would get caught, put down or even shot on the run. Surely, now he would stop coming back, bloodstained and ashamed, looking hunted when it was he was the one who was worrying Susie's sheep?

THE KILL

Screaming *Susie Susie* I ran up the ruined steps that led to nowhere and stood there with my hands in my mouth. I understood now what feathers flying meant. I was standing in a blizzard, Brownie's lupine jaws around their rust and white squawking necks. Why pick this moment? After all those evenings when he trotted by my side under the green beech tunnels, me in my red coat with my basket of eggs and canister of milk. Looking up brown-eyed and kind at Susie as she patted his rough coat. The yard was black with cars when I took a running leap from the crumbling steps throwing myself against the familiar high-latched door. Howling *Susie Susie Susie* bruising my hands against the wood. Darkness picking out the shadows one by one as everything became grey and quiet. Did he know that they couldn't stop in the middle or was Brownie able to gauge the exact decibel of prayer needed to drown out the sound of the kill?

GOODNIGHT IRENE

i.m. Irene Cotter (1919–2007)

Two words and I'm back
Burnfort Bar 1976 – the men have broken
into the raggle-taggle chorus
quit your rambling, quit your gambling
quit staying out late at night.
Mammy laughs *I won't be soft-soaped*
into doing after hours.

Further back, I'm small enough
to stand under the cold marble fireplace.
Mammy's not laughing, she's telling
about 1950. Every time it came on
her mother turned off the wireless.
Mammy was in Australia,
they never saw each other again.

If Irene turns her back on me, I'm gonna
jump in the river and drown. 2007. Lewes.
Martin Harley singing in the Royal Oak.
I stumble down the stairs onto Hill Street,
stand smoking under a full moon.
The song follows, a dog barks
and I can't turn anything off.

Suddenly I was awake.
I put on my petticoat with the three frills, yellow, pink and blue.
I tied the big pin on my mustard pleated kilt.
As I combed my hair in the grey mirror, I noticed the silence.
Down the stairs in my white bobby socks, treading softly
on the green-battleship lino.
It took me a while to figure out that they'd left without me.
I stood in the empty bar and the lager was dull gold in the dim light.
I couldn't believe it at first.
Didn't they know how much I was looking forward?
The Thomas Davis piper band out from Mallow
the waving of the green white and gold
the old IRA closing one eye to fire shots over the monument.
Years later, I saw shaky old men who could hardly lift their rifles.

Years later I saw shaky old men who could hardly hold their rifles.
The old IRA closing one eye to fire shots over the monument
the waving of the green white and gold
the Thomas Davis piper band out from Mallow.
Didn't they know how much I was looking forward?
I couldn't believe it at first.
I stood in the empty bar and the lager was dull gold in the dim light.
It took me a while to figure out that they had left without me.
Treading softly on the green battleship lino,
I came down the stairs in my white bobby socks.
I noticed the silence as I combed my hair in the grey mirror.
I tied the big pin on my mustard pleated kilt.
I put on my petticoat with the three frills, yellow pink and blue.
Suddenly I was awake.

WOODEN HORSE

'We're like the Greeks in the wooden horse, here in the belly of the town, I thought, and laughed.'

Ernie O'Malley

If you meet anyone, blindfold them: they were told that, and the men were smiling at the thought of seizing the barracks where an officer was starting to write a letter... *Mallow is a quiet town, nothing ever happens here.* And it was true – at 2 a.m. on the 28th there was no one on the streets, everything pitch-dark as they navigated backyards and barbed wire, put up their ladders against the high walls. Up there, Ernie saw a toy town wrapped in mist and when they clambered inside the Town Hall, he laughed, thinking of Troy. He whispered the story to Dave Shinnock who whispered it to the rest of the men and they never heard such a good joke and a boy slapped the thick wall and said *Now girl, whoa girl, steady there* and made a wind purr with his mouth as if he was rubbing down a horse, but Mallow wasn't made of wood, it was flesh and blood, like Achilles' horses, Bailius and Xanthus, who dragged their shining manes along the ground, crying for Patroclus.

MALLOW BURNS, 28TH SEPTEMBER, 1920

'The people of Mallow, long a garrison town, were not friendly.'

'The sheltering belly of our horse had paid for harbouring us.'

Ernie O'Malley, IRA Commander

9:30 a.m. and the sun passes over the steeple of St Mary's Church,
swans on the Blackwater, smoking men leaning against the Clock
House, women in brown hats buying milk in the creamery, skull-
and-crossbones badges flashing on the uniforms of the Lancers
exercising their horses along the Navigation Road as a solid gold
bar of dust breaks over Sergant Gibbs's khaki back and he bends
over the horse's hoof beside the blaze, the barracks quiet before the
rapid-fire of footsteps on the stone corridors when he turns from the
horse, hears the order *The Guard Room now, boys*, sees the trench-
coated men leading his comrades but he can't *Halt*, can't do it though
they say they'll fire and the first bullet goes through the sunbeam
and the horse shrieks and they shout *Halt* again and he shouts *No*
elongated and deep from his belly which is wet and sticky as his head
thuds against the jamb of the door and he smells something more
than horse sweat and someone tries to bandage him and then their
voices are faint, buzzing away and they have two Hotchkiss light
machine guns, twenty-seven rifles, one revolver, very light pistols, four
thousand rounds of ammunition, a quantity of bayonets and lances
packed in three motors in under twenty minutes and he won't hear
one of them playing a melodeon on the back of the car as they pass
out of the town into the safe countryside or the quiet all afternoon,
late sun falling on the black cloth of the Protestant minister and the
Parish Priest begging the Colonel in Buttevant for no reprisals and the
aeroplane that comes from Fermoy later again and circles over Mallow
Barracks and drops a message and flies to Buttevant before going back
to Fermoy and must be taking back the promise now because the sun
is sinking into the Blackwater and the Lancers are stone drunk and
they toss their cigarettes into the tide – a shower of loose red eyes
– and the people are nailing galvanised zinc in front of their plate-

glass windows and soldiers are driving in from Fermoy and Buttevant and the sun goes finally down on two hundred years of loyalty to the Crown, all night under the moon, the white swans on the black water against the red sky, screams, the creamery on fire, three hundred jobs gone, Town Hall flaming, houses alight, holy pictures bayoneted and one pregnant woman hiding beside the stones in the graveyard is too cold by the time the sun rises to ever get up again.

KNOCK

'Coughlin [...] helped to keep all in good humour, and his droll sayings were repeated. He had been billeted in a house which had a reputation for being stingy. One morning the woman of the house asked him how he liked his eggs boiled. "With a couple of others, ma'am," he replied.'

Ernie O'Malley, IRA Commander

No one wanted Ireland free more than myself. Don't I remember as a child my mother grabbing hold of us, making us lie down on the floor so we wouldn't be seen by the landlord out for his day with the ducks in the bog, his gun broken across his arm, looking to quench his thirst with a glass of milk. *I say! Very refreshing indeed* and a big slick of cream stuck to his old moustache. Ah those days are gone, thanks be to God, old Pym would be afraid of his life to come up to Knock in his plus fours now. That's what I was thinking this morning and how great it was to be able to open the bottom half of the door and stand out on the flags in my sack apron, the tongues of my boots hanging open. A brown cake baking in the bastable and the air tasting like lemonade. The sun going across my shoulders like a warm coat as I walked over to the henhouse with Blackie the cat pressing up against me. And I was walking out again with six hot white eggs in my big sack pockets, thinking of the breakfast I was going to have with Diarmuid when didn't I see a crowd of them coming round the corner with the old rifles upon their shoulders, singing *Oro Se De Bheath Abhaile* and my stomach sank to the tongues of my boots. Coughlin, the first as usual, to smell the brown cake. It wasn't that I wasn't wishing them the best of luck the whole time and you might think I'd be worried if we were caught out by the Tans and burned to the ground and I am not saying I wasn't always worried about that too, but to have to turn around and serve a crowd of men and make up beds and to have to pretend to be laughing away at their jokes... Oh God Almighty, I was pure sick of them all, then. I remember the first time they came and I was given a pile of dirty socks and Diarmuid handing the pile to me like it was a chalice, and I, like a mope, thinking it was some kind of an honour to be scraping the mud off them and when they were dry the next day, didn't I darn the lot of them like an even bigger mope. But this morning, anyway, I hid a couple of the eggs for ourselves and got a big pot of porridge going. 'Twas when Coughlin made his smart remark that I had to walk over to the fire because I thought I was going to cry and the only thing that cured me, as I was looking down into the bubbling oatmeal, was when I remembered being told how the waiters above in the Savoy Hotel in Cork might spit into the soup of a customer if they took a turn against him. And I am still smiling now through my stupid old tears, sitting by the well in the dark, thinking of what I've just put between our sheets after my old mope, Diarmuid gave our bed away to Coughlin for the night. Diarmuid, insisting, right go wrong, that it was a great honour and that nothing else would please me.

from

BURNFORT, LAS VEGAS

2014

BURNFORT, LAS VEGAS

for Martin Westwood

We move the Sacred Heart lamp
closer to Elvis's face now in the month
of June. I think that those
billboards of Vegas
could be the Major cigarette sign
or the Double Diamond Works Wonders
in the lounge window round '75
or the BP pump shining
in the blue Burnfort evening,
as the men come down
from the mountain and fill their vans
with petrol – a violet cloud
with a tantalizing smell and someone
says Burnfort is like New York
to those mountainy men the way
it is all built up with a school
and a church and a post office and us
city slickers running the pub,
shop and petrol pumps
and I believe it is true,
that we are like that to them –
there were stranger things then
to believe in, only now I think
it was more like Vegas, all those
signs, the games of forty-five
and my Elvis tape playing.
A few months ago
the novelty mug frightened us all
by spontaneously bursting
into *Viva Las Vegas* and I took that
as a sign, did what any
Catholic would do – put up a shrine.

MY DARLING CLEMENTINE

I never fail to see Daddy's hands
every time I watch *My Darling Clementine*
and this is often, as I love that film.
It's the point where Wyatt and Doc
might fight – first there's the whiskey
that Doc Holliday sends shooting down
the shining bar counter with the back
of his hand, followed by
a forty-five sliding up
from Brother Morg and sent sliding
down again before Doc and Wyatt
make their peace over champagne
and the whole room breathes
as men move back to the bar,
the conductor clicks his fingers
and the Mexican band starts to play.
I think of the story of Daddy suddenly angry
one night he had enough
and refused to be pacified with a drink
which he sent flying down
the Formica like Doc
with the back of his hand and that was
a funny anecdote to be told afterwards
the dramatic gesture so unlike him
and I think of his swollen crooked fingers
and how he was almost always powerless.
I am sure that no one was afraid for his life,
if there was a band, no way had it stopped
playing and the cowboys were drinking
steadily at the counter.
Daddy was more like Mack standing behind the bar
when Fonda asks, *Have you ever been in love?*
the small deferential bald head answers
subversively
No, I've been a bartender all my life.

GAZEBO

Gazebo was the word my mother
used to describe a mad exhibitionist
or a *queer hawk*. For example,
so-and-so *was going around*
like a right gazebo. Naturally I imagined
a gazebo had legs and travelled, so
I was surprised to see my first one
on an English village green, going
nowhere, the wedding couple
toasting each other under its rippling
blue and white canopy as cricket bats
smacked slowly in the heat.
My mother grew up near landed gentry
and the gazebos hidden in their walled gardens
must have entered her language
like escaped seeds,
growing into wild tramps
that straggled along the Rathkeale Road,
on strange, overblown feet.

DADDY AND MAE WEST

for my brother Richard Cotter, in memory of our father Richard Cotter (1902–1988)

Come up and see me some time, you said, patting the yellow Formica
with swollen crooked hands, the morning Mae died and Mammy
said there was more to you than met the eye, half laughing and half
annoyed too, as if Mae might have some claim on you. You were old
enough to be my grandfather and that wasn't always easy when you
were referred to as such and the truth is you didn't believe in washing
much maybe you were saving water for you were as pathologically
tight as a concentration camp survivor, knotted laces, rusty nails, old
Moore's Almanacs, the salvage fashion was waiting for you. Every now
and then there was a clean sweep and scrub and you were bereft as
I am now, reading my brother's email about the farm in the forties.
You sang but rarely to an audience, I remember *Fill Up Once More*
and *Glorio, Glorio, to the bold Fenian Men* but I was a child caught
up in days of wishing, why wouldn't you wash? My brother says that
your favourite was *Felons of Our Land* and he heard you sing *The Four
Leaf Shamrock* at Yellowtown, your tenor playing against a thick rapt
silence. You'd gone there to have a farm implement fixed. That word.
I hear you now frustrated in the seventies, asking had any of us seen
your *implement.* You used old expressions like *By Jove* and called bowls
vessels. But my brother saw you dancing – you. *Traditional ballroom
dancing* my brother writes and *he did the Russian Sailor dance, kicking
his legs while down on his haunches.* Come up and see me some time, I
want to say. Come dancing.

You'd always know people who never had anything, with the blowing out of them. You'd never hear the real gentry at that. Oh no, everything would be low key. No blowing. But everything good. Their clothes might be old but they were always good. Buy good and you'll save money in the long run. A quality material, like a good tweed, it never wears out. I remember Miss Finton in a herringbone coat, I saw her in the draper's with a piece of silk held between her fingers. I think she replaced the lining twice. There's nothing wrong with thrift, it's people who never had anything throw everything away. Of course, always have good gloves and shoes. Never without a pair of gloves, no matter what. Put the money into the shoes. When I see those ones going round in those scuffed white shoes – God, it looks very low, very cheap. And important to take care of the shoes too, polishing them the night before. Uncle Peter used saddle soap years ago. And always put the shoe-tree inside to hold the shape and don't have them thrown in a pile. And anyone who ever worked for the gentry became like them, close-mouthed. You wouldn't hear any old talk out of them. I remember one time old Liza Lawson came down with Tomeen, he must have been only two or three but he learned to talk very young. He used to be sitting up in the pram, like an old man holding conversations with people. Liza had taken him up to Lord Harrington's, wasn't she a maid there for the most of twenty-five years? And very well got by them too, they had great time for her and she even walked like them, so straight, you'd turn in the street to look at her but Tomeen must have seen something above at the Manor. Sure I don't know what he saw. Lord Harrington and the wife they didn't get on. Well, Liza was coming out in a sweat. As I said, anyone who ever worked for them became like them. Very close-mouthed. Loyal to the bone. She had to start waltzing Tomeen around the kitchen and singing over whatever he was trying to say. Tomeen must have seen Lord Harrington hitting, sure I don't know what happened only Liza was singing and going *wooh* up in the air with Tomeen and his hair flying straight up with the force and God, aren't I telling you, I couldn't hear what he was saying? I couldn't hear it. Did Lord

Harrington take a swing at the wife? Sure, I'm as wise as you. And anyway, they were gentry and they wouldn't like this kind of old talk and that's why Liza was so well got with them. She knew how to cover up and yes, you'd turn in the street to look at her. The shoes always well polished and a shantung coat of Lady Harrinton's altered on her. Good material. It saves money in the long run.

THE RECKONING

for Seeta Indrani

'For the Jews the Cossacks are always coming'

Linda Pastan

For my mother, it was the Bailiff.
I imagined him looking like Mrs Callaghan's
boyfriend who wore a cowboy hat
and cradled a big brandy on his beige thigh,
or maybe I'm mixing him up with the Sheriff.
My mother was afraid of him too.
The Sheriff was the Head of Taxes,
Mrs Callaghan was the lady accountant.
When she left town, the tax people
came after every one of her clients.
What a fool I was, my mother looked
into the hall mirror, her dark eyes
surveying the fool who'd stayed up late
filling Mrs Callaghan's glass, enthralled
by a woman who could be this
confident with everyone's money.
My brother-in-law did the accounts
after that, his curly hard-working head
bent over yards of white tape.
He wanted them to balance
but *How could they?* cried my mother.
We were openly and secretly eating
our way through the shop, inviting the cats
to join us in a big bonanza
of Rancheros, Aztecs and Coke.
We promised to tighten our belts,
would even have liked to lose weight
but soon it was Consulate cigarettes,
Huzzar Vodka, gallons of Maxwell House.

Fear of the Bailiff stayed with me though –
something in the blood because it couldn't be
the history book photos, there were
no cowboy hats in those pictures,
no affable Mrs Callaghan, no boyfriend
raising his ballooning brandy glass –
just black-shawled women, barefoot
children, RIC men with fixed bayonets,
the battering ram.

THE TRAVELLER

She came alone on foot
and straight away they noticed
she was a rebel; before punk,
before rap she had streaked hair
orange and black
and a loud transistor radio
that blared through the village
that hot day, drowning the sound
of the insects in the grass.
She didn't say ma'am to anyone,
she said, *I don't want your fucking*
ould clothes or your ould fucking
soft apples. She said she wanted money
and she went to every house
repeating her request, kicking foxgloves,
rejecting everything else that was offered.
And no one produced money, only
everyone said that the world had gone mad
and it was only now they realised
weren't the old tinkers lovely
and quiet compared to the cut
of that big one with her transistor
radio bawling under her arm like
a terrible fuck-you voice from the future.
The last place she called was Mikey Dorgan's.
He gave her a half dozen eggs
out of the goodness of his heart
not realizing that she meant business.
It was only when she'd left
he found that she'd pelted the six of them
and they were running in yellow streams
down the back of his gable wall.

ELVIS IS DYING

Well you may run on for a long time
Run on for a long time,
Run on for a long time
Let me tell you God Almighty's gonna cut you down

This Dalston winter morning I can stop time,
put down the biography
look out at the back garden where
the frost powders the vine twigs –
it's thirty-eight degrees in Memphis, he hasn't gone
to the bathroom yet. I take a look out
the front through frost-blackened
fuchsia – Balls Pond Road,
the woman in full adidas, the man in the truck tapping
the steering wheel, the seagull big as a cat.
When I pick up the book again
he's walking into the big red bathroom
with the black toilet, the chair in the shower. Ginger
sleeps through the Memphis heat, she will put on her make-up
before she checks on him, to the outrage of the eternal millions
crowding round the windows of Graceland
searching YouTube for his dappled shadow
flitting through that antebellum mansion. Behind
my grille of black twigs, I turn the page,
he's down in his face in his own vomit
and I remember his namesake,
that traveller from Cork, Elvis O'Donnell.
Strange to think, he died in a ditch the very same way.

SUBSTITUTE

'I think I could turn and live with animals'

Walt Whitman

She's talking about when she was a single mother. Like this is some calamity. I'm drifting because I've heard it before and then I have a sense of something unpleasant coming, there's something about not being able to get a man and then she's pointing at me, *Martina will understand me here, I got a cat instead.* I sit there, dumb as an animal thinking about how the four-legged ones don't point at you like that and I think of the Mater Hospital when I was twenty-four, just married and the doctor's breath so wine-rich every morning I just suffocated standing there, passing the cassettes. He said my rescue of the kittens born overnight in the warm cardboard X-ray files was *simple child substitution* and then I think of my father who had the full set of everything, a wife, six daughters and four sons, all at the same time but he is running, mad to get past us, running to the back door, running down the old cracked path as they stream out from every shed and hole in the hedge, from the fir trees and the galvanised roof tops and the warm felted boiler house, ginger, white, black, grey, fawn, their blended colours like a river of spices, spilling along the ground: Hamlet, Rolo, Tickles, Sputnik, Pompeius, Lunar and Gemini, Nuptials, Wardie, Mr 1972, Bimbo and he is shouting into the blue and white puffy Burnfort sky, like I shout now every time I return – *I'm back, I'm back.*

TOASTED CHEESE

for Fahima Sahabdeen

'Truly man is the king of beasts, for his brutality exceeds them. We live by the death of others. We are burial places [...] Endless numbers of these animals shall have their little children taken from them, ripped open, and barbarously slaughtered.'
Leonardo da Vinci, *Notebooks*

'Cheese digests all but itself. Mighty cheese.
   – Have you a cheese sandwich?
   – Yes, sir.'
James Joyce, *Ulysses*

Toasted cheese featured in one of my earliest picture books –
Granddad on the mountain toasting a slice on the end
of a long fork in an abridged edition of *Heidi*.
Daddy brought home strange lumps of leftover
rubbery stuff for the cats although they seemed
to prefer Cadbury's milk chocolate. I never stopped
to think where the never-ending stream of milk came from –
milk and whey was and is in everything
and especially at Rathduff Cheese factory –
stories of workers falling into outsize vats
like the giant saucepans of fairy tales,
these vats couldn't possibly be filled by the work
of homely milkmaids on three-legged stools.
The cruel river of milk came from elsewhere, like babies
and the queer dreams caused by eating cheese.

I'm thinking of toasted Emmenthal sandwiches –
the holey cheese reminiscent of cute mice in cartoons –
while reading Joyce's Lestragonians with whole-body prickling horror
and still envying broken-hearted Bloom
his Gorgonzola and Burgundy,
sitting up at the polished counter in Byrne's.
Take away that. Lubricate. A nice salad, cool as a cucumber.
Tom Kernan can dress. And Costcutters might sell Stilton.

Better to get it all over in one go,
stay up late tonight, for once and for all
eating everything on the cheese board.

But *meh*, Bloom said, *wretched brutes waiting at the cattle market,*
Staggering Bob – veal from a butchered tottering day-old calf.
To glug down his milk, one must believe his mother doesn't care.
The cows are waiting to be *pole-axed. Moo. Poor trembling calves.*
The Cotswolds, Easter 1999. Liadain got to milk
Buttercup, the single Jersey cow on a sheep farm
full of double-jointed jumping lambs, pure Eden
until we discovered Billy the calf with the chocolate curls locked
away in the dark. 'His mother's milk is too rich for him,'
the farmer was smiling at the soft city slickers. He hoped
for another Gulf War, he said war was good for the farmers,
it was evening when he said that and the sun
seemed to be shooting into the earth as he spoke.

And Billy cried as Buttercup lowed and looked picturesque
in the dusk like a romantic wrapper on a bar
of Swiss chocolate. Or one of those Anchor cows getting ready
to play football on a TV ad. And I can't stand any of it.
Packets of M&S sirloin
wrapped with pictures of dappled meadows and photos
of Honest John farmers. Bloom said it. We're all savages,
bad savages. If you can imagine cows
frolicking with footballs, then you must imagine their pain.
If the rich want to slobber in cruelty, don't make up stories
of happy *foie gras*, Fortnum and Mason.
Grandmother Cotter and the servants laughed indulgently
when Daddy cried for his calf going to market.
'Like a pure spoilt fool over animals all his life,' Mammy said.
Uncle Tommy was a proper man. 'And don't forget no one loved
horses more.' Tommy bred greyhounds for coursing,
maintained that to see a cat relaxing in a yard was a sign
the dogs were 'pure useless'.

It is tiring and painful, easier to let it go.
Like when the Brits accused the Boers of using dumdum bullets
which they invented themselves for India, the Boers said
they only used them on the blacks or the elephants
and everyone said okay then...
White missionary too salty, mutters Bloom
the outcast, ruminating on cannibals. *Like pickled pork.*
Expect the chief consumes the parts of honour. Cauls, mouldy tripes,
windpipes, faked and minced up. With regards
to the exploitation of cows, surely not, my sister
said in the old patronising voice,
Bubble and squeak. Butchers' buckets wobble lights.
Give us that brisket off the hook. Plup. Surely not, they said
when the Jews were melted down for lampshades
and soap. *Rawhead and bloody bones. Flayed glass-eyed sheep hung*
from their haunches, sheepsnouts bloodypapered snivelling nosejam
on sawdust. Top and lashers going out and still I'm heading
for the door, ripping up the zip of my parka,
stopping to tie my shoelaces tight when

'A minute on the lips, forever on the hips,' says
another disembodied voice from the seventies.
I go out into the crisp-leaved October night, not seeing
the amber-glowing copper beech on Balls Pond Road
but windowless artificially-lit factory-farm sheds, hiding
in the dark countryside. *Peace and war depend*
on some fellow's digestion. Religions.
Christmas turkeys and geese. Slaughter of innocents.
Eat, drink and be merry. Then casual wards full after.
Heads bandaged.

Kneel for a while with the fruit jellies,
peering at the tiny print – it's gelatin in every bag and
the E120 in Skittles comes from the Brazilian cochineal insects
boiled alive. 70,000 make one pound of *natural* cochineal
stain and the sweets are still seduction red.
Am I pure spoilt too like Daddy?
What about big Brazilian families with mouths to feed?

Mouths, mouths, and worst of all, *the hungry famished gull*
of my own mouth now. I buy four Mr Tom
Turkish peanut brittle bars, eat them all in one go,
still thinking of Bloom and his Gorgonzola.
Splintering Mr Tom between my teeth,
I try not to think of other nights of temptation
streaming out ahead of me as I watch *Taking Root,*
a documentary about Wangari Maathai
and her Kenyan women, getting over Colinisation,
planting trees. Later, I dream that I've joined the *Mau Mau,*
wake late in a room full of sun with hungry cats
poking at me. One more day, a murderer reprieved.

THE DAWNING OF THE DAY

after Roisin Tierney, *Dream Endings*

The first time I drew back
the curtain in the newly bought Dalston wreck,
I heard the clopping of hooves
and there it went – a glass coach with four
black horses and plumes – the corpse, the casket,
the coachman wearing a high hat.
I didn't know about East End funeral carriages,
then they became a regular sight, disappearing
into Our Lady and St Joseph's Catholic churchyard
with their *Mum* and *Dad* wreaths or once a piper
in a plum velvet cloak stopping traffic
as he played *The Dawning of the Day.*
But the shiver still comes back
when I pick up Roisin's *Dream Horses*
and at the same time hear
the hooves on the stone outside.
Someone is *getting the feathers* again – makes me stand
still at the old floor-length windows that
wouldn't pass *Health and Safety* now. The past
is a heavy breath on Balls Pond Road –
the endless vein of oyster shells in the earth,
the ancient wind-up window shutters
coming up on a pulley.
The fear of being buried alive
inclines me towards cremation
and the garden would be the right place
for a scattering, along with Marcel, Eileen
Murphy and Alice's kittens.
Fitting when I have worked so hard to fertilise
that piece of ground. It's a comfort
and a horror every time I hear the coach clatter.

ON THE BORDER

for Joanne and Tony

Balls Pond Road has the cream
of sunsets. Rubbish, boarded-up
squatted buildings, heavy traffic that grinds
and grates under the piercing call
of police cars and over it all clouds,
turquoise, salmon, shell and navy.
My eyes search for each landmark of home:
the plane trees, the big copper beech, the almshouses,
and the recording ghost of Jerry O'Neill
landlord at The Duke of Wellington.
He stands on his flat roof
looking out over Hackney to the East,
Islington to the West and I've lived with his words
for weeks. His poetry of London
and the thrust of this poorest of places
in the sixties and seventies
is both a familiar and queer
last glimpse of a disappearing world.
I can't take my eyes off his empty roof.
When it grows dark, I garden by electric light,
exchanging tulip bulbs for old oyster shells
in the sticky earth while the traffic like an angry sea
echoes and booms through the grubby cliffs
of our yellow-bricked buildings.
Later, I will scrub my earthy fingernails,
rinse my hair from a jug as I sit
in the cast-iron tub unglamorously bolted to the floor.
The bath trembles when the lorries rumble by,
reminds me that Georgian bricks aren't cemented
so everything keeps shifting.

THE MYSTERY OF SHOES

I avert my eyes passing
shoeshops
but the devil peers out,
ruby eyes illuminating
a window in Venice
filled with expensive colours
of chocolate, donkey, desert.
Mary Magdalene unbuckling
Jesus's dusty sandals,
all those people in the Bible
showing off their toes,
the gleaming shoes my daughter begged for,
smart as paint, strapped to her feet,
they made her shy, so chic
she was afraid that they'd speak to her.

THE PRICE OF SHOES

Shoes speak to Liadain,
her bedroom floor carpeted
with pink high heels, rusty soft
moccasins, red strappy peep
toes, papery worn Robin Hood
boots fixed with PVA glue.
There are ghosts too,
the yellow stilettos I refused
to buy when she was twelve.
Her tiny frame
and big smile balanced
on top of those long lemon tongues
You can't have them because –
the air so scarce and hot
in Tammy's changing room
it made me blurt –
they're like something a prostitute would wear!
The black Doc Martens were heroic –
they kept her warm and dry.
She could run fast in them.
The last day of school
Hampstead Heath swells
with drunken teenagers,
and one shiny tobacco-coloured
brogue is lost in the hawthorn.
But I don't share her grief.
I feel relief
as if the shoe is a coin
paid to the wild
for her safe return.

I WANT TO BE LIKE FRANK O'HARA

but I've never leaned
on a club doorway listening
to Billie Holiday. Most of my time
in this city I've been a mother and I know
I've spent too much time in Sainsbury's
Dalston branch even if it does
have its own inimitable vibe
and a huge range of root vegetables.
My own roots sink deep in the garden and
I can't bear to leave
in case I miss a single bloom
or one of those odd powder-blue butterflies
passing through on its way to Hackney Marshes.
I swing in the hammock to the sound of police sirens,
but I've never leaned on a club doorway,
my poems in my pocket like Frank.
My books are stuffed with shopping lists
and I can't believe that's Frank.
Although once at 11 a.m. looking
for the new GP surgery in Green Lanes,
I stuck my head in the doorway
of a Turkish men's club and they scattered
from their chess like leaves.
I felt a bit dangerous then, like Elvis in '56.
I think Frank would have liked it,
the way one brave man approached me slowly,
his hands out in front as if
he was about to catch something.

PUTTING IT ON

In the convent secondary school
Sister Benedicta – also known as *Big Ben* –
said I was *putting it on. Acting.*
I didn't know what she was talking about
until copper-haired, brown-eyed Dolores
stood up for me. *She can't help it, Sister,* Dolores said
but Dolores wasn't listened to either when she
tried to explain that I'd learned to stand like that
in National School.
I'd carried it over, unconscious of how
annoying it was for the nuns,
me with my one hand clutching the desk,
one bottle-green-stockinged leg braced against
the iron rung underneath, the other
stuck out in front, ready to run.

THE SLAP

In the insanity of that room with its dirty mushroom-
coloured walls, when he unrolled the rattling blank map,
cranking himself up as he watched
our blind-mole fingers trying to trace the path
of the *Broad Majestic Shannon* or the boundaries
of the *Rebel County of Cork.* In that one half of a two-
roomed schoolhouse his tall desk creaked
as he leaned over it, his green eyes burning,
his legs in their paper-sharp creased trousers
flying up behind in a dance. We watched
Ronan Shea's six-year-old head
put into a motorcycle helmet,
the crown of it over his face
or Ray Twomey kicked in the stomach
with a balletic brightly polished shoe. But when it came
to slaps, he never held our hands, we were allowed
to try and move our palms to save our fingers.
It was The Game and you had to have Nerve
but we were small and frightened
and the day he held Bernardine Logan by her
delicate-boned sensitive-redhead's wrist,
a tremor went through us, the captive audience.
I see his spittle-face of triumphalism
thrust up against her titanium
white features, after she tried to stand up to him,
and the turntable of my stomach is unstoppable now
although it is years since she died
and he's long rotten.

THE PROMPT

Was he thinking aloud or trying
to help? If we had to stand up to spell
a word *as Gaeilge*, he croaked along with us
and that was all we had to go on with –
tossed every day
on the storm of sounds, the unintelligible language
that must have been beaten *out* of children
on the same spot a hundred years before
a language filled now with pain and spittle
and because he stuttered
in between the letters, his 'uh' and 'eh' and 'ah'
could be taken for the wrong vowel,
the signal for him to dash
to the drawer for his stick.
We rocked in front of him, our ears
cocked to his tobacco breath,
another game of bluff.

SUPERVISED STUDY

Eugie gets off her high chair
at the top of the study and paces
between our desks, Sister Mary
Eugenius has the bluest eyes and
she walks like a man, like she's never
cared for her own good looks.
She puts the fear of God
in the girls yet she likes me, thinks
I'm good at French. Her subject.
Four brown-papered textbooks
are carefully arranged in what I call a *quad*
over Mario Puzo's *The Godfather.*
I jolt when she pauses by my desk,
attracted by *French Verbs*
ostentatiously displayed on the left.
On top, another textbook, *Maupassant.*

Once, Guy was another secret read,
resting on my knees under the desk
with one eye on the Master. At ten,
the weirder the story, the better
I liked it but now I've moved on
to the Sicilians.
Eugie groans with delight
as she plucks *Maupassant* from the desk,
Quelle histoire? Ah,Vendetta – très intéressant!
I blush, it must have passed for shyness,
The Godfather is nakedly displayed
on my desk but she does not see it.
Eugie's glad, she tells me, to see
I'm finally settling down
making full use of my God-given ability.

ANATOMY LESSON

I've still got my *head in the books*
sucking the clandestine comforts.
I'm twenty and Professor Coakley
jerks his knee like a whip of rope
demonstrating muscle movement
at the top of the class. It's *Tess*
this time hiding under
Kitty Clark's Positioning and others.
Thomas Hardy is morbid enough
for me all right and when the girls sit
forward, I know I'm missing something
interesting about muscles or is it tendons?
I'm sure now that I'm *doomed* to be always holding
the wrong book. The pretty Opus Dei celibate
struggles excitedly through the door
with the rattling skeleton, *Oh Professor Coakley!*
She is called a Numerary, there are rumours
she wears a spiked chain around her thigh.
On top, she is definitely wearing
a desert-coloured Prada sweater, her hair
cut in a perfectly symmetrical shining
brown cap, her face deeply red
before the distinguished Professor.
I hate the way the other girls
look at her, smile and exchange looks.

FLOWERS IN THE ATTIC

I hate Dublin and the radiography lectures
and the X-ray department even more,
they laugh at my Cork accent and one
of them said *Aids is a North Side disease.*
I don't want to be here with the snobby girls
with the Donnybrook accents or the registrar
who has nicknamed me *Cork* even though
he is kind. The girl who loves sailing
asks every single one of us what
our fathers do – owning a pub
sounds like something dirty now.
Alone for a moment, I crawl into the shower
with *Flowers in the Attic* and a cinema-sized
bag of Maltesers. Minutes later, Sister
Patricia taps on the door. She smiles
at her fellow Corkonian. I know she cycles
the underground corridors of St Vincent's
in the dark evenings, her white veil flying.
I know she knows a fellow oddball.
Now, Tina.
I hide my trashy book behind my back.
*When you've wiped your face, you'll
have to come back to Nuclear Physics.
The Siemens engineer's been in there
for the last five minutes.* I'm nearly twenty-one,
scared I'm pregnant,
no qualifications, no hope yet,
mournfully following her white habit.

LONDON IRISH

for Marcella Riordan

If I could sing and play the piano
I would like to sit down to thump out
that profound ballad Finnegan's Wake.
Welt the flure your trotters shake – if you sing that
line often enough to yourself
you get a bit of handle
on Joyce's big shake-up of the English
language. No harm at all to feel around
in the dark of your head and see what
comes out. Piling up chickpea flour
at the Madina Store, Mohanlal reaches out
with a lollipop
for Liadain and calls her *baby*
and we laugh even though I know
he knows that's what she is to me –
how did Liadain become twenty?
As we hurry to the vet with ginger Donny
in his comfy leopard-print bag bought online
under the banner – *Live the cappuccino
life-style!* – an Irish wino catches up with
us at the lights. We all stand together
at Dalston Junction and he brandishes
his can like a diviner:
*ha ha dee, has the ould fella
deserted ye for William Hill,
is he down below in the pub?*
He knows he's spot on
we're on our own
and we don't have to say anything
only laugh again
as the lights change
and we rush on with Donny roaring.
The man twirls like a leaf stuck
to the lamppost, calling after us
that he sees the *Irish* in our faces.

THE GREEN STORYBOOK

for Fiona

Today, the first edition – 1947 – with fine
cross-hatched illustrations arrives from eBay,
in a cellophane-covered never-before-seen
dust wrapper. The apple-coloured
jacket was long gone by the time
The Green Storybook fell into my chubby hands
in the sixties. I taught myself to read
from that book, Enid Blyton's distinctive
script running across the darker green cloth cover.
I would look for her again and again,
the *Secret Garden* door,
that first Royal Flush, the miracle
of the black marks straightening themselves
out into sense across the page,
saying this way, this way
you'll escape.

NOTES

His Master's Teeth | Page 40

Bowling (pronounced to rhyme with 'howling') is an ancient Irish game played along country roads in Cork and Armagh. The small metal bowl is thrown along the road and there's a lot of gambling on the winner, that is whoever gets to the finishing line in the fewest throws.

Two Hostages | Page 73

The Black and Tans were a mercenary military police force sent by Lloyd George in 1920 to put down the Irish rebellion. They drove special trucks known as Crossley Tenders.

The Rabach | Page 54

'Rabach' is the Irish for violent or vigorous, both of which are appropriate in this case. The Rabach lived on the Beara Peninsula in the early nineteenth century. *Pluais an Rabach* translates as Cave of the Rabach.

INDEX OF TITLES